DK Eye Wonder

Bugs

LONDON, NEW YORK, MUNICH,
MELBOURNE, AND DELHI

Written and edited by Penelope York
Designed by Janet Allis

Managing editor Sue Leonard
Managing art editor Rachael Foster
US editors Gary Werner & Margaret Parrish
Jacket design Chris Drew
Picture researcher Jo Haddon
Production Kate Oliver
DTP designer Almudena Díaz
Consultant Paul Pearce-Kelly

First American edition, 2002

04 05 10 9 8 7 6 5 4

Published in the United States by
DK Publishing, Inc.
375 Hudson Street
New York, NY 10014

York, Penelope.
  Bugs/by Penelope York.--1st American ed.
  P. cm. -- (Eye Wonder)
  Summary: Describes a variety of insects and their behavior,
  discussing metamorphosis, camouflage, defenses, and their
  benefits to people.
  ISBN 0-7894-8552-4 -- ISBN 0-7894-8553-2
  1. Insects--juvenile literature. [1. Insects.] I. Title. II. Series.

QL467.2.Y67 2002
595.7--dc21

        ISBN 0-7894-8552-4
        (ALB) 0-7894-8553-2

Color reproduction by Colourscan, Singapore
Printed and bound in Italy by L.E.G.O.

see our complete
product line at
www.dk.com

Contents

Bugs, bugs, bugs

Most of the bugs that you know are called arthropods, which means they have their skeleton on the outside of their bodies. There are over a million known species of arthropods on the Earth. Here are a few types to spot.

Trapped in time

We know that insects were around over 40 million years ago because some were trapped in a substance called amber, which hardened back then.

Thorax

Head

Abdomen

What is an insect?

You can spot an insect by counting it's body parts and legs. They all have six legs and three body parts – a head, a thorax, and an abdomen.

What is a myriapod?

If you try counting the legs on a creepy crawly and find you can't, chances are you are looking at a myriapod, such as a millipede or centipede. They have lots of segments and lots and lots of legs!

Extreme bugs

- The petroleum fly lives in puddles of crude oil and feeds on insects that get stuck in it.

- Some midges can be put into boiling water and survive.

- Snow fleas can survive in sub-zero temperatures. If you pick one up it will die in the heat of your hand.

What is an arachnid?

All arachnids have eight legs. Watch out however, other than spiders, a lot of arachnids look like insects so count carefully.

What is a true bug?

These days we tend to call all creepy crawlies "bugs" – as we have in this book. But actually a true bug is a type of insect that has a long mouthpart that it pierces its food with, and uses it to suck up the inside of it.

Leapers and creepers

Some bugs are speedy, some are slow. Some bugs run and others jump. They all have their reasons why they do what they do, and a lot depends on where they live – different obstacles demand different types of movement.

High jump
The flea is the most powerful jumper of all insects. It has a little spring in its legs to enable it to jump very high. It can jump 600 times an hour for three days, when it is looking for a host.

Legging it

The green tiger beetle is the fastest insect on earth. It runs at 3 1/2 ft (1 m) per second. It uses its speed to catch other insects and to run quickly across the hot desert sand.

Leaps and bounds

If a grasshopper or cricket is disturbed and it needs to get away, it uses its massively developed, muscle-packed legs to leap high into the air.

A grasshopper can leap 20 times the length of its body

Looping upward

Some caterpillars loop their way up branches. They attach their back leg suckers to the branch and stretch their bodies forward, then loop up their back, pulling the suckers upward. They can walk up some pretty steep twigs.

Keeping in step

A millipede has up to 180 pairs of legs! They all help it force its way through the soil. It has to be very coordinated when it walks, otherwise its legs bump into each other. It moves them in waves.

Up, up, and away

Creepy crawlies are the ultimate explorers; they can get anywhere and everywhere. This is because many of them have wings. Flying insects have two pairs of wings but use them in different ways. All, however, are experts in aerobatics.

Lift off
The lacewing flutters gracefully using all four wings. It can control each pair separately, which means it can turn easily and even fly backward.

Flutter by
The butterfly flaps all its wings at the same time at about five beats per second. It's wings are delicate and it has to be careful that it doesn't damage them.

Gone in a flash!
The little hoverfly can beat its wings up to 1,000 times per second. Sometimes it flies too quickly to be seen. It hovers in the air then darts away so quickly that it seems to disappear.

Haltere

Cruise control

The second set of wings on flies have turned into halteres that look like drumsticks. The fly uses these for balance and coordination, and they help the fly to change direction in a split second.

A hard case

The beetle only uses one pair of wings to fly. Their front wings have become hard cases that protect the flying wings when they are folded away.

THE INCREDIBLE JOURNEY

When the winter cold arrives in the Rocky Mountains, the monarch butterfly migrates up to 3,000 miles to the finer weather in California and Mexico. This insect covers 80 miles (129 km) a day and travels in huge groups. At the end of their journey they always settle on the same tree as the year before, and no one knows how they find their way.

Making sense

Imagine being able to taste with your feet, or having eyes as big as your head. Sounds odd? Well bugs have some pretty strange ways to find their way around and sniff each other out.

Feeling the way

Some insects, such as this cave cricket, live in dark places where there is little light. Because of this their eyesight is not good. Instead they use long feelers, or "antennae," which stop them from bumping into walls all the time in the pitch black.

Powerful perfume

Antennae are also used to smell. This male moth has two hairy antennae that can smell a female moth from $6^{1}/_{2}$ miles (11 km) away!

A matter of taste

This butterfly tastes with its feet. When it lands on a particularly tasty flower, its long mouth-parts, or "proboscis," unfold automatically and allow it to drink.

Bending your ear

Bug's ears can be found on their wings, bellies, or heads; and believe it or not, this katydid (bush cricket) listens with its knees! The slits on the legs are ears that can pick up other cricket's calls.

Bug-eyed
The horsefly's enormous eyes take up almost all of its head. Its eyes are very sensitive to movement, which is why it is so incredibly difficult to swat.

Meat eaters

There are so many bugs around, you would have thought it would be easy for predators to catch and eat them. Wrong! Hunters have to invent cunning ways to get their dinner, and have weird ways to eat it, too.

The waiting game

A praying mantis hides camouflaged among leaves where it sits still for a very long time with its forelegs ready to strike. When an insect passes, it pounces at lightning speed and chews it up in its jaws.

Wrap it up

The spider waits patiently in its web for an insect to fly into it. It then wraps the bug up in a jacket of silk to stop it from moving, injects it with venom, and then sucks out its insides.

Dragonflies need a lot of wing skill to catch a bug in flight.

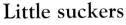

It takes the orb web spider about an hour to spin a web

Fast food

Hawker dragonflies are so nimble and speedy that they can catch insects in midair. They grab a passing insect with their powerful jaws and grip it with their long legs.

Little suckers

The assassin bug is a typical piercer and sucker. It catches its prey then pierces the body, injecting saliva to turn the inside of the prey into liquid. Then the assassin sucks it dry.

The trapdoor spider spends most of its life waiting for its next meal.

Knock knock!

The trapdoor spider makes a hole for itself underground and weaves a trapdoor of soil and silk. When an unsuspecting insect wanders over the door the spider is out like a shot to snatch it and gobble it up.

Cunning carnivores

● The Portia spider from Australia taps on the webs of other spiders pretending to be a fly. When the spider arrives to eat the fly, Portia eats it up!

● The ant lion larvae buries itself in the ground with its mouth facing the sky. When an ant runs over it, it falls straight into its jaws and is eaten swiftly.

Bug veggies

Most bugs in the world are vegetarians and munch like crazy during their short lives. Some are piercers and suckers, and others are biters and chewers; but however they do it, they do it a lot.

Army of eaters

Caterpillars are big eaters. They are biters and chewers and have to nibble constantly in order to grow into adults. They have powerful jaws and strong teeth that can chew through tough leaves.

Liquid lunch

When the caterpillar grows into a butterfly it turns into a piercer and sucker. It feeds on liquids, which it sucks up using its long, hollow tongue (the proboscis), like a straw.

Heavy duty chewing

You may find wood tricky to eat, but this stag beetle larva doesn't. It chews and chews rotten wood until it is fat enough to turn into a beetle.

When butterflies and moths are not hungry, they roll their tongues into tight, curly coils.

The acorn weevil only eats acorns and is an unusual eater. It pierces the hard nut with its long snout, and chomps away inside with the jaws it has at the end of it. It then sucks the food up the snout into its body.

This weevil also lays its eggs in acorns

Now you see me...

Lurking in the undergrowth there are many bugs that look like bugs, and many bugs that don't. Cunning camouflages help some bugs to catch a meal and others to avoid becoming one.

Spiky survivors

Birds are not going to risk landing on a prickly branch, so what better disguise than to look like a spiky thorn – as long as these treehopper bugs keep still.

Flower power

If you look carefully at these beautiful flowers, you will be able to work out the shape of an orchid mantis. It can change color from white to pink to blend in with the particular flower that it chooses to sit on.

Lost among leaves

As long as this leaf mimic katydid sticks to the right leaves, it definitely won't be spotted. It even has veins on it's back just like the real leaves have.

Dropping in

Yuk, that bird dropping doesn't look very good to eat. Wrong – it's actually a very tasty king swallowtail butterfly caterpillar.

Twiggy

At first glance it is just an innocent looking twig. Look again. This walking stick insect makes sure he doesn't come to a sticky end.

Playing dead

Look closely at these dead leaves – one of them is very much alive. The cryptic moth sits on the decaying leaf and is almost invisible. No one is going to spot it there.

MOTH STORY

Once in England there lived a pale colored peppered moth that hid against the light colored bark on trees. By the late 19th century the moths mysteriously started to become darker. Eventually it was realized this was because the pollution from the factories had darkened the trees. Only the darker moths remained camouflaged, and they were the only ones that survived.

Warning signals

Some bugs make it obvious to their attackers that they would be nasty to eat. They make it known in various ways "Don't eat me or you'll be sorry." Others have methods that startle hunters, and a few use clever disguises.

Snake scare

It may look like a snake, but it's actually a caterpillar! This crafty creature is safe from hunters. Who would risk eating a snake?

Making eyes

Imagine taking a quick glance at this little banana eater butterfly. You'd think that those eyes were on a much bigger and more ferocious beast.

Hot bomb

A bombardier beetle under attack has a deadly revenge. It squirts a chemical out of its butt at high speed and at a temperature of nearly 100°C!

Ultimate defense

When attacked, the puss moth caterpillar rears up its colorful head. Bright colours warn a predator that a bug is poisonous so they leave it alone.

Weta whack

Disturb the enormous weta cricket and you are in for a shock. Quick as a flash it shoots its back legs up to give a sharp kick.

Copycat

Some bugs are lazy. They are not poisonous so they copy the colors of something that is, and they are left alone. Can you tell the difference between the bee with a sting and the harmless hoverfly? No? Good disguise! The bee is on the left.

Mother care

Most creepy crawlies lay their eggs and abandon them to fend for themselves. Others make sure that the eggs will hatch on their first meal, and a few make very good moms indeed.

Doomed!

The parasitic wasp lays its eggs on a live caterpillar, which can't shake them off. The caterpillar continues getting fatter and juicier until the eggs hatch out and gobble him up. A yummy first meal!

Born alive

The aphid is a weird breeder. It gives birth to live young – unusual for an insect – and doesn't even need to mate with a male to give birth. If they all survived, one aphid could produce billions more in six months. Luckily lots of bugs eat the aphids or we would be overrun!

Protective shield

The mother shieldbug looks after her young with great care. Sometimes she glues them to the male's back for him to take care of until they hatch! When they are born she guards them fiercely.

An aphid being born.

Piggyback ride

The jungle scorpion is a very good mom. She gives birth to live young, catching them as they are born, and puts them onto her back for two weeks until they are strong enough to fend for themselves. She can carry up to 30 babies at a time.

All change

Some insects start their lives looking completely different from their adult shape. When they are ready, certain insects, such as caterpillars, have a sudden change and emerge with a new image. Others change slowly and steadily.

1. Caterpillar stage
The blue morpho butterfly starts off as a small, hairy caterpillar, which eats and eats and eats until...

2. Pupa stage
...it sheds its skin and creates a pupa. A transformation happens inside, and one day...

3. Emerging
...the pupa splits and a completely new-looking insect starts to emerge. It pushes itself out until...

4. Butterfly
...it stretches out its crumpled wings and flies away as a beautiful butterfly. The change is called metamorphosis and happens to many creatures in the insect world.

Skin shedding

Some insects change slowly as they grow up, such as this dragonfly. Because insects have their skeletons, which don't grow, on the outside of their bodies, it means that they have to replace their skins in order to grow bigger. This dragonfly is shedding its skin for the last time.

Buzzing around

If you hear a buzzing sound in your yard, chances are you are listening to something that stings, such as a bee or a wasp. But there's more to these buzzing bugs than meets the eye. They build some incredible homes and are excellent team players.

Collecting nectar

During the spring and summer, the honeybee flies from flower to flower to gather nectar. Back in the hive the nectar is used to make honey.

A hive of activity

Honeybees live in hives. Inside the hive they make a honeycomb, which is made out of wax from their glands. The six-sided cells that make up the honeycomb hold honey and eggs, which the queen bee lays.

Bee dance

When a worker bee finds a good nectar supply, it returns back home to the hive and does a little "figure eight" dance, which lets the other bees know where the nectar is.

PAPER MAKER

There is a legend in China that the inventor of paper, Ts'ai Lun (AD 89-106), watched wasps while they made their paper homes and copied them. He chewed and chewed pieces of wood in the hope that he could make paper. Unfortunately it did not work well, so he swapped saliva for glue and invented the paper that we still use today.

Building a nest

Some wasps live in large nests made of paper. The queen wasp starts the nest by chewing dead wood, mixing it with saliva, and letting it dry. She then lays some eggs, which hatch, and the next generation continuing with the nest-building.

Sweet tooth

Wasps love sugar and especially sweet fruits, which is why they buzz around your food in the summer, annoying you. They won't sting you, however, unless you threaten them.

Army of helpers

Ants and termites each live in huge colonies where they build their homes together, work together, and never have time for play. Their whole life revolves around bringing up their young safely.

Loyal subjects

The queen termite is a huge, ugly, egg-laying machine that never moves from her royal chamber. The termites rally around her, feeding and cleaning her.

Termite high-rise

Some species of termite live in huge mounds that they build using soil, saliva, and their droppings. The mounds can be up to 20 ft (6 m) high.

The king termite lives with the queen in her nest.

Big bully

The toughest ant around is the Australian bulldog ant. It grips its meal in its huge, powerful jaws then swings its body around and stings the prey from behind. Bugs that get in his way don't stand a chance!

Firm friends

Ants and aphids are very good at keeping each other happy. The aphids eat a lot of tree sap and give off a sweet liquid that the ants like to sip. In return the ants guard them fiercely from predators.

Lots of bugs like to eat aphids, so having ant bodyguards is the best way for them to survive.

THE ANT CLEANING SERVICE

Every so often villagers in Africa receive visits from a march of up to 22 million driver ants, which forces them out of their homes. Although each ant is only $1/3$ in (1 cm) long and blind, they kill every pest that gets in their way, such as locusts and scorpions. The villagers welcome the clean up!

Teamwork

Some ants build their nests by weaving together groups of leaves. They each carry a live ant larva in their jaws and make it produce silk, which they then use to sew up the leaves. If anyone threatens the nest, they attack by biting.

Deep in the jungle

Nobody knows how many species of bugs there are in the jungle. New ones are being found all the time, which means that there are a lot more to be discovered. The ones that we do know, however, are pretty odd.

Big head

The lantern fly gets its name from its very long head, which sticks out of its body and has a bright end on it. Some lantern flies (which are actually bugs, not flies) are huge, with a wingspan of up to 6 in (15 cm).

Giant of the jungle

The giant tiger centipede is very large and aggressive. It runs at high speeds across the forest floor, using its many legs. It eats other bugs and sometimes even toads, lizards, or small mammals.

Queen of flight

The Queen Alexandra's birdwing is the largest butterfly in the world, and one of the rarest. It's wingspan can grow to 11 in (28 cm).

Tiny spiny

The postman butterfly caterpillar has sharp spikes all over its soft body, which protect it from predators. It feeds on poisonous passion flower leaves that are absorbed into its body and make it poisonous, too.

Hairy, scary spider

During the day, the red-kneed tarantula sleeps in its silk-lined burrow. Then, when it starts to get dark, it emerges for the night hunt searching for large insects and injecting them with venom.

Sand devils

The desert is a tough place to live. Not many plants grow there and there is little water around. Bugs need to be pretty sharp if they are going to survive one of the hottest places on earth.

Honeypot pantry
The honeypot ant workers feed other honeypot ants with lots of nectar, which they store in their huge tummies. When food is scarce the ants with the pot-bellies vomit up the honey that they have made and feed it to the workers.

Jewel of the desert
The jewel wasp is solitary – it doesn't live in a swarm. Here it is stinging a cockroach that it will lay its egg on. A first tasty meal for its youngster.

The store ants spend all their lives hanging from the ceiling

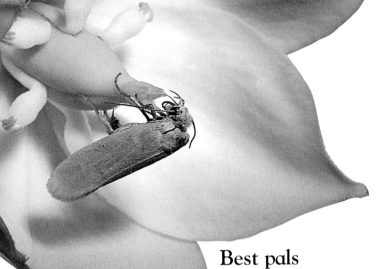

Best pals

Without each other, the yucca moth and the yucca plant wouldn't survive. The moth lays her eggs on the plant and in return pollinates it as she does so. The newborn caterpillars eat the seeds, but leave enough for new plants to grow.

Dew drinker

The darkling beetle has a slick way to find its drink. It waits until the morning when dew has formed on its back, then leans forward and catches it as it trickles into its mouth.

A sting in the tail

This desert scorpion hardly ever needs to drink. It gets most of its moisture from the spiders and insects that it eats. Its sting is so poisonous that it could kill a person.

Desert carpet

Large swarms of these desert locusts eat in the cool of the night and rest during the day's heat. Sometimes, there are so many that they look like a huge desert carpet.

Water world

If you find a body of water, chances are it's filled with minilife – but you may have to look closely to see some of it. Many bugs live in or above the water, and some can even walk on the surface.

Diving in

The diving beetle is the great meat eater of the water. It tucks a bubble of air under its wings so it can breathe underwater, and dives down to catch tadpoles and even small fish.

Walking on water

Pond skaters can walk on water because of thick, waterproof hairs on their feet. They skim over the surface looking for floating food.

Darting around

The beautiful dragonfly lives above water. It is called the dragonfly because of its very aggressive "dragon-like" behavior.

Bottoms up!

Mosquito larvae live in the water. When they need air, they swim to the surface and hang there with their snorkel-like breathing tubes poking up through the top.

Back stroke

The water boatman hangs upside down just beneath the surface. It looks like a little boat, and its back legs are just like oars, which is how it got its name.

Caddis armor

The larva of the caddis fly builds a case around itself to protect it. It makes the case out of stones, shells, and pieces of plants.

Watery web

The air-breathing water spider makes a diving bell to live in. It weaves a web under water, among the plants, and stocks it with air from the surface.

Little mites

This house dust mite is 0.001in (0.3 mm) long and eats flakes of your dead skin. You have millions of dust mites in your home, which live in mattresses, furniture, and carpets. They can cause people to sneeze and wheeze.

House mites

You may try to forget that bugs live all over your home, but the fact is they are there. They may not all be nasty, but they have one thing in common – they like living with us.

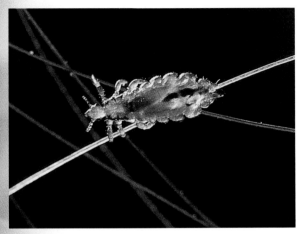

What a louse!
Once a female head louse has a tight grip on one of your hairs, she is very difficult to get rid of. She can lay 50 eggs (nits), each at the base of a single hair. She causes your head to itch because she sucks blood from your scalp.

Spiders in the home
The house spider likes to live in dark places in your home, such as down the drain. Sometimes you will spot it scuttling across the floor to eat flies and other bugs.

Fly alert!
Flies love to share the food you eat. They vomit their digestive juices onto your meal, which turns it into liquid that they suck up into their bodies.

Unwanted guests
Cockroaches are badly behaved visitors. They eat anything tasty they can find in the home and once settled are very difficult to get rid of.

As dusk falls...

As day turns into night, some insects are just starting to wake up. Whether they are trying to keep from being eaten, or getting ready for a meal, night is a pretty lively time in bug land.

Moon moth

The first time it flies, the Indian moon moth takes to the air after dark to avoid being eaten. It doesn't have a mouth because it only lives long enough to survive on the food it ate when it was a caterpillar.

The spider also holds its net in the air, ready to catch insects.

Light fantastic

Fireflies and glowworms use a special organ in their tummies to flash light signals in order to communicate with each other. Sometimes hundreds gather together to attract mates, and can be seen for miles, like the ones in this tree.

Web master

The netcasting spider weaves its fatal net before dark. Then at nightfall it hangs upside down and drops it on any delicious insect that wanders past.

Glowworm

Glowworms are not worms, they are beetles. This female glowworm cannot fly. It glows all the time to attract insects to its light so that it can catch and eat them.

Dark stories

● The cicada's clicking sound can often be heard at dusk. It has a flap under its stomach that clicks loudly at very high speeds.

● Moths are attracted to artificial light because they use the Moon to navigate and confuse lights with the Moon.

Weird and wonderful

There are so many bugs that have evolved mysterious habits and strange looks that they could fill a whole book. Here is a small selection from around the world.

How weird would it be to have eyes on the end of stalks?

Eyes on stalks

The eyes of stalk-eyed flies are on the top of long stalks. When two males meet they compare eyes and the one with the widest set gets the girl.

Terrifying taste

The flambeau butterfly has very strange taste in food. It sits on an alligator's eyes and sips its tears. What a very brave little bug.

Stick your neck out

Why does the giraffe weevil have such a long neck? No one knows. But it certainly makes it one of the weirdest looking bugs.

Mystical mantis

You can barely tell which way around this mantis nymph is facing. If you look carefully, however, you can just see its head on the right-hand side. It's strange coloring helps it to camouflage itself.

Out of this world
If you came across this katydid (a type of bush cricket) in the jungle, you'd be forgiven for thinking that we'd just been invaded by aliens, with it's spiny body and strange colors.

Pests and plagues

They may be small, but bugs can do a surprising amount of damage, in large numbers or on their own. Humans sometimes have to try hard to control them, and very often we lose.

Leaping locusts

Imagine a swarm of a billion locusts. Yuck! A swarm this big, which we call a plague, can eat every crop in a region in a matter of hours. When there are so many locusts together at once, they blot out the Sun as they pass overhead.

Colorado killer

In 1850, settlers arrived in the Rocky Mountains and they brought with them the potato. These tiny Colorado beetles got a taste for potatoes and swept across the United States eating the whole crop. They are still a serious pest.

Deadly skeeter

The deadly mosquito is the world's most dangerous animal. It can spread a disease called malaria when it sucks blood, and has been responsible for killing more humans than any other living creature.

Only female mosquitos drink blood.

It's all in the kiss

The kissing bug likes to suck blood from near a human's mouth. It leaves its droppings near the bite, which can get scratched into the skin, resulting in an illness called Chagas' disease.

Big sucker

This tsetse fly is filled with blood that it has just sucked out of a human. But not only does it leave an itch, it can also leave behind a deadly disease called sleeping sickness.

A DEADLY TALE

In the past, when someone old was dying, their relatives sat up with them all night to watch them. Often the sitters would hear an eerie tap, tap, tap coming from the wooden walls. It was a small beetle that eats through wood. When it hatches from its egg it bangs its head against the wood to attract another beetle to it, making a tapping sound. That's how it got its name – the deathwatch beetle.

41

Cleaning up

Nature has its own recycling service in the form of bugs that feed on dead plants, animals, and dung. Left uneaten, the remains would build up into a huge pile of rotten gunge. We should be very thankful for these small cleaners!

Feeding frenzy
Maggots are the specialists on eating decaying flesh. Flies lay their eggs on rotting animals. The eggs hatch into maggots. Their stream-lined shape helps them to bury into the flesh to eat it.

Great balls of dung
When a pile of dung appears in Africa, the dung beetles rush in, each one claiming a piece of the action. The male makes a perfect ball of dung and rolls it away and buries it. The female lays a single egg in the ball and when it hatches, the beetle grub eats the dung.

Cleaning agents

Millipedes live in damp, dark areas
and are very useful cleaners. They
eat any rotting leaves and dead bugs
lying around, breaking them down
to become part of the soil again.

DUNG DISPOSAL

When Europeans arrived in Australia, they brought
cows with them (there were none there already).
The dung beetles in Australia were used to dry
kangaroo pellets, not the soft cowpats, and
the pile of cowpats got larger and the flies
got worse until an answer had to be found.
So the Europeans introduced African dung
beetles to Australia which were used to soft
dung. The Australians now enjoy a fast rate of disposal.

The essential bug

Whether you like them or not, bugs are an essential part of our lives. We spend a lot of time trying to get rid of them, but we could not live without them.

Lick it cricket

About 500 types of insect provide a good, healthy snack for people around the world. These crickets give these lollypops a good crunch to look forward to.

Honey bee

Without bees helping to pollinate by moving pollen from flower to flower, we wouldn't have nearly as many plants as we do. Bees also supply us with endless amounts of sweet honey.

Silky threads

Did you know that when you wear silk you are actually wearing material made by a caterpillar? When the silk moth caterpillar pupates, it makes a silk lining for its cocoon, which we use to weave into cloth.

Pest control

Sometimes insects, such as these aphids, multiply so quickly that they eat huge amounts of our crops. The best way to get rid of them, wihout poisoning, is to introduce other insects that eat them, such as the ladybug.

This is known as biological pest control

Glossary

Here are the meanings of some of the words
that are useful to know when learning about bugs.

Abdomen the rear part of an
insect's or spider's body. It holds all
of the main organs of the animal.

Amber clear brownish-yellow liquid
from ancient pine trees and that
hardened millions of years ago.

Antenna the delicate feeler on an
insect, which is used to smell, touch,
or hear. An insect has two antennae
on its head.

Arachnid an arthropod with eight
legs. Spiders, scorpions, and mites
are all arachnids.

Arthropod an animal with jointed
legs and a body divided into
segments, covered by a hard outer
skeleton. Insects, arachnids, and
myriapods are all arthropods.

Bug a true bug is a type of insect
that has a long mouthpart that it
pierces its food with in order to
suck up the inside.

Camouflage colors or patterns that
help bugs to blend into their
surroundings so that they are hidden
from view.

Colony a group of bugs, all in the
same species, that live and work
together to survive.

Crop a plant that is grown and
harvested by humans.

Decay the rotting of plant or animal
matter by the action of bacteria
or fungi.

Dew the moisture that forms on
cool surfaces overnight.

Disease an illness that can cause
extreme sickness or even death.

Disguise changing the way you look
in order to look like something else.

Dung the natural waste of animals.

Gland an organ in a body that
produces a special substance.

Grub the baby of an ant, bee,
wasp, or beetle.

Haltere one of a pair of drumstick-
shaped structures that are found on
flies. They are the second pair of
wings, which help the fly to balance.

Hive the home of honeybees.

Host the animal that provides a home for bugs, such as fleas or lice, who live off it.

Insect an arthropod with three body parts and six legs.

Larva the very young stage of an insect that looks completely different from its parents.

Metamorphosis the change from young to adult in an insect that looks completely different to its parents.

Migration moving from one place to another to live for a while, most commonly to find better weather.

Myriapod a type of arthropod with many legs, such as a centipede or millipede.

Nectar a sweet liquid found in many flowers.

Perfume a pleasant-smelling liquid that attracts a type of animal to it.

Plague a group of insects that is out of control and causes trouble.

Pollination when tiny grains fertilize female plants in order to produce seeds and grow new plants.

Pollution dirty gasses and waste from factories and cars that make the air, land, or water unclean.

Predator an animal that hunts other animals for food.

Prey an animal that is hunted by other animals as food.

Proboscis a tubelike mouthpart used by some insects to suck up liquid food.

Pupa the hard case in which some young insects completely change to become a different adult shape (during metamorphosis).

Recycle to treat materials in such a way that they can be used again.

Saliva the watery liquid, which is in the mouth, that helps to digest food.

Solitary being or living alone.

Swarm a mass of bugs, such as bees or locusts, that stick together to eat or find a new home.

Thorax the part of the body between the head and the abdomen on an insect. The legs and wings are attached to this part.

Vegetarian bugs that survive by eating just plants and no meat.

Venom a poison that is injected into another animal to paralyze or kill it.

Web a structure of fine silk threads spun by spiders to trap small bugs in.

Wingspan the measurement from one wing tip all the way to the other wing tip when they are fully stretched out.

Index

Acknowledgments

Dorling Kindersley would like to thank:
Dorian Spencer Davies for original illustrations;
and Sarah Mills for picture library services.

Picture credits:

The publisher would like to thank the following for their kind permission to reproduce their photographs:
a=above; c=center; b=below; l=left; r=right; t=top;

BBC Natural History Unit: Bruce Davidson 42cla; Premaphotos 27bl. **Densey Clyne Productions:** Densey Clyne 47br. **Bruce Coleman Ltd:** Jane Burton 14cra; Andrew Purcell 32bc; Kim Taylor 35bl. **Corbis:** Anthony Bannister/Gallo Images 44bl; **Michael & Patricia Fogden:** 20tl;

Michael Freeman 44cr; Dan Guravich 3. Michael & Patricia Fogden: 16ca; 31tl. **Frank Greenaway:** 29tl. **N.H.P.A.:** Anthony Bannister 31tr, 38cla; 37bc; G I Bernard 20-21; Mark Bowler 17ca; Stephen Dalton 6cra, 6-7, 8clb, 8crb, 8-9, 13cra, 35tr, 35cla; Daniel Heuclin 40cl; Stephen Krasemann 18tr; Haroldo Palo Jnr 38tr; Peter Pickford 26; Dr Ivan Polunin 36-37. **Natural History Museum:** 22-23, 48cra. **Oxford Scientific Films:** Katie Atkinson 27tl; G I Bernard 33bl; Jack Clark 5, 45c; Fabio Colombini 2; S A L Cooke 41tr; Satoshi Kuribayashi 18cla, 24tl; London Scientific Films 23; Mantis Wildlife Films 37tr; L Martinez 13tr; Paulo de Oliveira 7tl; Tim Shepherd 15. **Papilio Photographic:** Robert Pickett 22cla. **Premaphotos Wildlife:** Ken Preston-Mafham 17tr, 19, 38tl. **Science Photo Library:** Darwin Dale 37tl, 41cla; Eye of Science 34; Dr Morley Read 39; Nuridsany & Marie Perennou 44cl; David M Schleser/Nature's Images 16-17; Jean-Philippe Varin/Jacana 30tl; Kazuyoshi Nomachi 40-41; Art Wolfe 17tl; Paul Zahl 13bl. **Telegraph Colour Library:** Hans Christian Heap 28cla. **Woodfall Wild Images:** Andy Harmer 13cla; Peter Wilson 14tl; David Woodfall 8-9. **Jerry Young:** 4c.

Jacket: **Bruce Coleman Ltd:** Kim Taylor **Michael & Patricia Fogden:** Michael and Patricia Fogden. **Premaphotos Wildlife:** Ken Preston-Mafham **Jerry Young**